I want to be a teacher.

I like to help.

I want to be a banker.

I like to learn.
I want to be a good student!

What Will I Be?

by Corrina Villegas

NATIONAL GEOGRAPHIC   **Hampton-Brown**

National Geographic and the Yellow Border are registered trademarks of the National Geographic Society.

National Geographic School Publishing
Hampton-Brown
www.NGSP.com

Printed in the USA.
RR Donnelley, Crawfordsville, IN.

ISBN: 978-0-7362-7996-3

16 17 18 19   10 9 8 7

Acknowledgments and credits continue on the inside back cover.

I like to help.

I want to be a doctor.

I like to help.